How Do You Train a Goldfish?

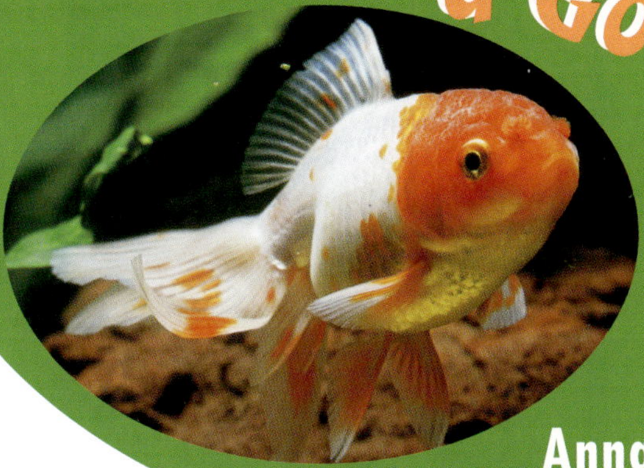

Anna Ciddor

800-445-5985 www.etacuisenaire.com

How Do You Train a Goldfish?

ISBN 978-0-7406-1567-2
ETA 305051

ETA/Cuisenaire • Vernon Hills, IL 60061-1862
800-445-5985 • www.etacuisenaire.com

Published by ETA/Cuisenaire® under license from Pearson Education Australia
(a division of Pearson Australia Group Pty Ltd)
All rights reserved.

Text © 2001 Anna Ciddor
Designer: Andrea Jaretzki
Acknowledgments: Cover, 3, 4–5, Gerard Lacz/ANT Photo Library; 6, 14–15, 24, 28, Jean-Paul Ferrero/Auscape; 7, 11, Otto Rogge/ANT Photo Library; 8, 20–21, N.H.P.A./ANT Photo Library; 9, Klein/Hubert-Bios/Auscape; 12, Stephen Saks/photolibrary.com; 13, Yves Lanceau/Auscape; 16–17, Renee Lynn/Photo Researchers Inc.; 18–19, Australian Picture Library/Corbis; 22–23, Andrew Henley/Auscape; 25, Silvestris/ANT Photo Library; 26, Ralph Reinhold/photolibrary.com; 27, Tegan Park Labradoodle Breeding & Research Centre; 29, Getty Images.

No part of this publication may be reproduced, stored in a retrieval system, or transmitted, in any form or by any means, electronic, mechanical, photocopying, recording, or otherwise, without the prior written permission of the publisher.

Printed in China by QP International Ltd

08 09 10 11 12   10 9 8 7 6 5 4 3

Pet Quiz

How do you train a goldfish?

What do you feed a pet snail?

What pet grows legs after it is born?

Where can you find a chocolate cat?

If you don't know the answers to this quiz, you'll have to read this book! It's full of funny questions and answers about pets.

How do you train a goldfish?

You can train your goldfish to know when it's feeding time. Try this trick...

A Bell Means It's Feeding Time

You will need a bell. Every day, put the fish food in the same corner of the fish tank. Ring the bell before you drop in the fish food. When the goldfish hears the bell, it will learn to swim to the feeding corner. You have trained your goldfish to know it's feeding time.

What do you feed a pet snail?

You can feed fruits and vegetables to your pet snail. Snails like leafy foods. They like carrots, lettuce, and celery, but make sure they're fresh!

You should also wash any fruits and vegetables you give your snail. Fruits and vegetables from the store are sometimes sprayed with poison that kills snails!

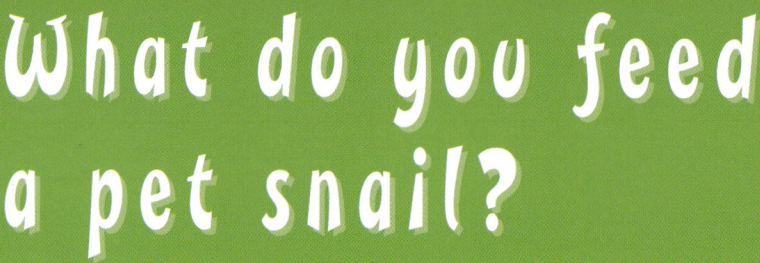

Snail Munchies

If you are very quiet when your snail is eating, you might hear it munching on its food!

Where can I get a snail?

You can find a pet snail in the yard. Look under stones or leaves. It's best to look early in the morning or in the evening.

What pet grows legs after it is born?

When tadpoles are born, they don't have legs. Tadpoles are baby frogs. They have long tails that help them to swim. Tadpoles live in the water like fish.

Tadpoles begin to grow legs. Their tails get shorter. When they turn into frogs, they want some dry land!

Where can you find a chocolate cat?

You know that cats come in many colors. But you probably don't know some of the funny names for these colors.

A dark gray cat is called a blue cat.
A light gray cat is called a lilac cat.
A dark brown cat is called a chocolate cat.

So, if you want to find a chocolate cat, look for one that's dark brown!

What pet likes to swing?

Pet mice like swings. They like having their own playground where they can climb, crawl, and swing. You can make a playground for a pet mouse.

A loop of string makes a good swing for a mouse.

A cardboard tube makes a tunnel for mice to crawl through.

A piece of string is fun for mice to climb.

A thread spool is good for a mouse to roll on.

What other things could you use for a mouse's playground?

Try This

It's a good idea to put a "gnawing log" in a mouse's cage. A mouse's teeth are always growing. Mice like to gnaw on the wood log to stop their teeth from getting too long.

What pet dog will fit in your backpack?

A chihuahua will fit in your backpack. It might even fit in your pocket!

A chihuahua is the smallest pet dog in the world. Most chihuahuas are only about 5 inches tall. Chihuahuas weigh only $4\frac{1}{2}$–$6\frac{1}{2}$ pounds.

Chihuahuas used to be called pillow dogs. This was because their owners let them sleep in their pillows to keep them warm!

What pet should never have a bath?

A hamster should never have a bath. If a hamster gets wet and cold, it can get sick and possibly die.

Hamsters don't need baths to stay clean. They spend a lot of time cleaning their fur. Their fur contains oil that keeps it clean and healthy.

Is it a bear or a hamster?

There is a type of hamster called a Black Bear! It's a long-haired hamster with black fur.

What pet is a good gardener?

You could say that a pygmy goat is a good gardener because it likes to eat weeds! Pygmy goats like to eat the weeds that other animals don't like.

In autumn, you don't have to rake up the leaves because pygmy goats like to munch on the fallen leaves, too!

Young male goats, called billies, are not very good gardeners. They attack trees with their horns! While they tear off the bark, the billies are sharpening their horns.

Would you like to have a hundred pets?

If so, what you need is an ant farm!

Pet Collecting

You can collect ants in a jar. Carefully place the jar near an anthill. Put some dead insects inside the jar. This will help attract the ants.

Keeping All Those Pets Happy

You can give your pet ants some dead insects to eat. They also like sugar and water mixed together, or honey mixed with water.

Tiny Pets

To enjoy these tiny pets, you might need a magnifying glass to see what they are doing!

What's the difference between a pony and a horse?

A pony is a small horse. A pony is usually less than 60 inches tall when it is full-grown. You can ride a pet pony.

The Shetland pony is between 32 and 48 inches tall, and has a thick mane and tail. Shetland ponies come from the Shetland Islands, off the coast of Scotland. That's where the name comes from!

The only foods ponies eat are grass and hay. They're easy to keep happy!

This is a Shetland pony and its baby foal.

What pet fish can walk?

Fish called axolotls can walk. These fish have specially shaped fins that they use like legs!

Walking fish need water, so they can be kept in a fish tank. Put some sand in the bottom of your tank, and it can be the land they walk on!

Axolotls come from Mexico. That's why they are sometimes called Mexican Walking Fish.

Fish Bites

It's probably not a good idea to put smaller fish in with your axolotl. The axolotl will try to eat them! You can feed walking fish some small pieces of fish a few times a week.

What pet needs a dentist?

You need to check your guinea pig's teeth once or twice a year. Like mice teeth, guinea pig teeth keep growing. If their teeth get too long, it is hard for them to eat. Guinea pigs need a block of wood to gnaw on. This is how they file their teeth.

This guinea pig is chewing on wood shavings.

Flowers for Your Guinea Pig

Nasturtiums and sweet peas are two kinds of flowers that guinea pigs eat.

What dog makes a good pet if you're allergic to dog fur?

If you are allergic to dogs that shed, then a poodle is the dog for you. Most dogs don't need their fur cut. But a poodle's fur keeps growing, so it needs to be cut, or clipped.

Did you know?

The Labradoodle is a cross between a Labrador and a poodle. It's a good guide dog for blind people with allergies.

How can you make your pet turtles race?

Draw a large circle with chalk, then put the racing turtles in the middle. The turtles will start walking at their usual slow pace. Sometimes they might even stop!

Don't push or turn the turtles. You can try to help them move by offering them food. The first turtle across the line is the winner.

Remember to be gentle and nice to your pet turtles.

Fast Turtles

Not all turtles are slow creatures. The green sea turtle below can swim almost 20 miles per hour.

One type of soft-shell turtle can sometimes go faster than a human...as long as the ground isn't too bumpy!

Glossary

allergic   sensitive to something; get sick from it

billies   billy goats or male goats

file   smooth down by rubbing or chewing

fins   the thin flat parts of a fish's body that help it to swim

gnaw   keep biting on something that's hard

horns   the hard parts with sharp points that grow out of the heads of male goats

Labrador	a large black or light brown dog
magnifying glass	looking at things through this glass makes them bigger
poison	something that can hurt or kill living things
pygmy goat	a small goat
train	practice doing a task
wood shavings	thin pieces scraped off of a piece of wood

Index

ants	18
axolotls	22, 23
billies	16
cats	9
chihuahua	12, 13
dogs	12, 13, 26, 27
frogs	8
goldfish	4
"gnawing log"	11
green sea turtle	29
guinea pig	24, 25
hamster	14, 15
horse	20
Labradoodle	27
Mexican Walking Fish	22
mice	10, 11
pony	20
poodle	26, 27
pygmy goat	16
Shetland pony	20, 21
snail	6, 7
tadpoles	8
turtles	28, 29